Political & Economic Systems

FASCISM

David Downing

www.heinemann.co.uk/library
Visit our website to find out more information about Heinemann Library books.

To order:

 Phone 44 (0) 1865 888066

 Send a fax to 44 (0) 1865 314091

 Visit the Heinemann Bookshop at www.heinemann.co.uk/library to browse our catalogue and order online.

First published in Great Britain by Heinemann Library,
Halley Court, Jordan Hill, Oxford OX2 8EJ,
a division of Reed Educational and Professional Publishing Ltd.
Heinemann is a registered trademark of Reed Educational and Professional Publishing Ltd.

OXFORD MELBOURNE AUCKLAND
JOHANNESBURG BLANTYRE GABORONE
IBADAN PORTSMOUTH (NH) USA CHICAGO

Designed by AMR
Illustrated by Art Construction
Originated by Dot Gradations
Printed in Hong Kong by South China Printing

ISBN 0 431 12433 7 (hardback)
06 05 04 03 02
10 9 8 7 6 5 4 3 2 1

British Library Cataloguing in Publication Data

Downing, David
  Fascism. – (Political & economic systems)
  1. Fascism – Juvenile literature
  I. Title
  320.5'33

Acknowledgements
The publishers would like to thank the following for permission to reproduce photographs: AKG: p. 37; Corbis: pp. 30, 33, 39; Hugo Jaeger/Timepix/Rex Features: p. 5; Hulton Archive: pp. 6, 8, 9, 11, 12, 14, 19, 20, 22, 24, 29, 31, 35, 42, 45, 46, 48, 52; Popperfoto: pp. 16, 26, 27, 50; Report Digital: p. 55.

Cover photograph:General Franco salutes troops at a victory parade in Madrid, 27 May 1939, reproduced with permission of Corbis.

Every effort has been made to contact copyright holders of any material reproduced in this book. Any omissions will be rectified in subsequent printings if notice is given to the publishers.

Our thanks to Christopher Gibb for his comments in the preparation of this book.

Disclaimer
All the Internet addresses (URLs) given in this book were valid at the time of going to press. However, due to the dynamic nature of the Internet, some addresses may have changed, or sites may have ceased to exist since publication. While the author and publishers regret any inconvenience this may cause readers, no responsibility for any such changes can be accepted by either the author or the publishers.

Contents

Any words appearing in the text in bold, **like this**, are explained in the Glossary.

1 Images of fascism

A group of men in brown or black shirts are walking down a street at night. They might be carrying guns, but more often than not they have only knives, broken bottles, clubs, or brass knuckles. They are looking for political enemies to beat up, not to kill, though of course accidents will happen. A socialist or a communist would be best, but anyone who disagrees with them will do. This is the way these men conduct their politics, in all the villages, towns and cities of their country.

After several years of this, there is a meeting in some government office. The country's old rulers – the upper classes, the conservative politicians, the big businessmen – are talking to the leader of these so-called fighting groups, these gangs of thugs who have taken over the streets. If we give you power, they say, will you bring back law and order? The leader promises that he will.

A few months later, he strides up the steps of some huge arena, surrounded by thousands of armed and uniformed men. Blazing torches light the night sky, roars of adoration and enthusiasm fill the air. The leader speaks, shouts, screams at his audience. The only subjects of his speech are his country's greatness and its need to settle accounts with all who try to hold it back. The crowd howls its agreement, and the stadium shakes to the stamping of a hundred thousand boots.

A few more years and the tanks are rolling, the dive-bombers swooping out of the sky. The leader struts through some foreign capital, admiring the architecture, enjoying his triumph.

Another few years and his own cities are in ruins. He dies, killed either by himself or his own people. And the ghastly truth begins to emerge, the camps full of skeletons, the millions who have vanished for ever.

These images tell the story of fascism. Images in themselves, however, explain little. Why did so many people vote for parties which were little more than gangs of bullies? How did those gangs organize their state, their economy, their people's work and leisure time? Where did their racism come from, and why did they risk everything in war? Why, above all, did they become the greatest mass murderers of modern history?

A torchlight parade of Adolf Hitler's followers, through the German city of Nuremberg in November 1938.

Where did fascism come from?

Fascism was born in Italy and Germany in the years after World War I, which ended in 1918. In both countries terrible economic hardships were accompanied by feelings of bitterness and betrayal. Italy, though on the winning side, received much less from the peace settlement (the **Treaty of Versailles**) than had been promised. The defeated Germans were forced to give up a large amount of territory and to pay reparations (huge fines) for starting the war – punishments which many people considered neither fair nor wise. Italian and German soldiers returned from the war to find their countries in the middle of an economic crisis. It seemed as if they and their friends had suffered and died in vain. Their nations were far worse off than before, and it was hard to find jobs to feed their families.

Broken societies

In Italy, Benito Mussolini's Fascist Party managed to seize power by the end of the post-war economic crisis, but their German counterparts – Adolf Hitler's National Socialist Party, or **Nazis** – needed the second chance offered by the **Great Depression** of 1929–33. In both countries the basic situation was the same. Economic crises had split the nation from top to bottom.

German troops chase communists through the streets of Berlin during the failed revolution in the winter of 1918–19.

The rich and powerful were mostly able to ride out the storm. The working classes turned, in the main, to **socialism** or its new, more extreme variant, **communism**. But the middle and lower middle classes – the millions of **white collar workers**, small businessmen, teachers – had nowhere to go. The rich would not help them, while socialism and communism threatened to drag them down to the level of the **blue collar workers**. **Inflation** had taken their savings, unemployment was a constant threat, and the streets were full of armed and angry men. **Democracy** had failed them. What they wanted was someone to impose order, to put things right, to mend their broken societies. Fascism grew out of this desire. What the middle classes desperately wanted was for someone to recreate a sense of national unity, by force if necessary.

Ideas which inspired fascism

Of course, human history is littered with examples of **dictators** who claimed that their countries needed strong leadership for one reason or another. Many have considered themselves **nationalists** – that is, people who have not only put their own nations first, but also regarded their own nations, in some usually unclear way, as being superior to other nations. In the 20th century such violent nationalism often went hand in hand with another **right-wing** attitude, violent anti-communism.

Such notions – some might call them **ideologies**, others might see them as little more than prejudices – were important elements of fascism. Both Mussolini and Hitler were violent nationalists and anti-communists.

Some of the other ingredients in fascism's mixture of ideas were even more vague. The Nazis were very impressed by a group of late 19th and early 20th-century thinkers called the Social Darwinists.

Charles Darwin, in his book *The Origin of Species,* had put forward his theory of evolution, arguing that those species which best suited themselves to their environment were the ones that survived. The Social Darwinists, much to Darwin's horror, applied this theory of the survival of the fittest to human societies. The Nazis took from this the idea that the strongest nation deserved to win the biggest prizes, that might was right. They were also attracted to ideas put forward by the German **philosopher** Friedrich Nietzsche, who preferred the idea of strong leadership by a 'superman' to a democracy which reflected the interests of the less educated majority.

One writer who was supposed to have influenced Mussolini was the French thinker Georges Sorel. In his book *Reflections on Violence*, Sorel welcomed violent action and argued that a leader should use large, dramatic ideas and plans to inspire the masses. Mussolini certainly glorified strength and violence, and was always ready to paint exaggerated pictures and make unrealistic promises, but he probably did not get such ideas from Sorel. It is much more likely that Sorel's book simply provided him with a justification for doing what came naturally.

Benito Mussolini as Italian Prime Minister, flanked by bodyguards, December 1922.

The same could be said of Hitler's supposed influences. The philosophical ideas which he and the other **Nazi** leaders took from the Social Darwinists and Nietzsche were those which gave their existing prejudices an air of respectability. In the end, there were no great or profound ideas behind fascism. As Mussolini himself said, 'It was born of a need for action, and it was itself from the beginning practical rather than theoretical.'

Two men

The men who filled this need for action, who showed the necessary daring and took the necessary risks, were important to the success of fascism in the 1920s and 1930s. Mussolini and Hitler were both extraordinary men. As public speakers, they were able to make their promises of social unity and new national success believable to large numbers of people. As political leaders, they were more ready than most to lie and cheat their way towards their goals, completely unrestrained by any belief in the worth of a human life.

Adolf Hitler (centre, in raincoat) and other Nazis at a remembrance service in Nuremberg, September 1928.

Fascism, or something very like it, would doubtless have existed without Mussolini and Hitler. Its mixture of nationalism, anti-communism and strong leadership seemed, for a time, to offer the only way out for the hard-hit lower middle classes of Italy, Germany and several other European countries. The fascism which actually came to power in these countries was deeply influenced by the two leaders' particular experiences and personalities.

Neither Mussolini nor Hitler had much time for the upper classes. Indeed, both men were full of resentment for how they had been treated before they came to power, when they were nobodies. They were not **reactionaries** who were resistant to change. Unlike the Spanish fascist leader General Franco, they had no desire to live in the past. They thought of themselves as **revolutionaries**, and they considered fascism a revolutionary idea, one that would shake up, inspire and ultimately strengthen their respective nations.

FOR DETAILS ON KEY FASCISTS, SEE PAGES 59–60.

Fascism: the word

In the time of the Roman Empire, magistrates (legal officers) carried a bound bundle of sticks (*fasci* in Latin) with a protruding axe head to symbolize their authority. Mussolini revived both the word and the symbol in 1919. His party, followers and fighting groups took the name Fascist, and the bound bundle of sticks became their logo. Hitler's followers in Germany called themselves National Socialists rather than fascists, but the two movements, as Hitler himself wrote in a letter to Mussolini, were fundamentally similar.

3 Taking power

Italy

In order to gain power, fascists used both intimidation and persuasion. The intimidation came first. In Italy Mussolini organized *squadristi* or fighting groups which terrorized both towns and countryside. Armed with daggers and long wooden clubs, the *squadristi* would roam the streets looking for enemies to beat up. They would often force people to drink castor oil to make them vomit, and sometimes chain them naked to trees. Anyone who spoke out against such violence was putting his or her life at risk.

Early in 1921 the Italian fascists formed themselves into a proper political party and began trying to convince people that they had the right policies for the country. The intimidation continued, but promises were now added to the threats. The rich were offered an end to the threat of **socialism** and **communism**, the middle classes were guaranteed order. Even the working class was offered something. In its early days, fascism borrowed many of socialism's policies, like taxes on wealth, a minimum wage and more government control over industry. All classes were promised a revival of national pride.

Italians were offered a choice: more and more violence or something for everyone. Not surprisingly, many chose the latter. When, late in 1922, Mussolini organized a March on Rome by his fighting squads, it seemed easier to make him prime minister than fight him.

Benito Mussolini (centre) during the 'March on Rome'. In reality, Mussolini and these other leaders did most of their travelling by car or train.

11

Germany

In Germany's southern province of Bavaria, the small German Workers' Party used much the same tactics and offered much the same policies as Mussolini's fascists. This party, which soon changed its name to the National Socialist German Workers' (**Nazi**) Party, was founded by Anton Drexler in January 1919, but within a year its dominant figure was an Austrian veteran of the German army named Adolf Hitler.

Like Mussolini, Hitler set up a private army – the brown-shirted **SA (Sturmabteilung**, or stormtroopers) – with the aim of intimidating his political opponents. Like the Italian Fascists, the German National Socialists tried appealing to all classes, adding one policy which was close to Hitler's heart – **anti-Semitism**. The Jews were blamed for everything that had gone wrong: Germany's defeat in the war, the greed of big business in a time of economic crisis, the spread of communism.

Unlike Mussolini, Hitler refused to make use of the democratic process. In November 1923 the National Socialists tried to seize power by force in the Bavarian capital, Munich, and were swiftly defeated. Hitler was sent to prison, where he wrote his autobiography and political manifesto, *Mein Kampf (My Struggle)*. When he was released late in 1924 the economic situation had greatly improved and people were less inclined to listen to him and his party.

A lorryload of Nazi stormtroopers in front of Munich's city hall during the failed uprising of November 1923.

It seemed as if the German fascists had missed their chance, but five years later the Great Crash on Wall Street ushered in the years of the **Great Depression**. This time Hitler pursued party politics alongside the street-fighting and bullying, and it paid off. By July 1932 the National Socialists were the largest party in the **Reichstag** (German parliament). The leaders of Germany's political and industrial elite then took the same gamble that their colleagues in Italy had taken. They tried to buy off a fascist leader by offering him power within their system. Hitler was appointed **Chancellor** of Germany in January 1933.

No holds barred

'The Brownshirts (SA) were lunging toward the centre of the hall, to fall upon the intruders. A terrifying mêlée [confused fight] followed. Blackjacks, brass knuckles, clubs, heavy buckled belts, glasses and bottles were the weapons used. Pieces of glass and chairs hurtled over the heads of the audience. Men from both sides broke off chair legs, and used them as bludgeons [clubs]. Women fainted in the crash and scream of battle. Already dozens of heads and faces were bleeding.'

(German writer Jan Valtin describing events at a political meeting addressed by Hitler's deputy Hermann Goering, in the years before the Nazis came to power)

Elsewhere in Europe

Many other countries were badly hit by the Great Depression, and many other fascist parties sprang into existence, hoping to repeat the successes in Italy and Germany. The most important of these were probably the Legion of the Archangel Michael (later the Iron Guard) in Romania and the Arrow Cross in Hungary, both of which posed a real threat to their respective governments during both peace and war.

FOR DETAILS ON KEY FASCISTS, SEE PAGES 59–60.

None of the fascist movements in the West – like Oswald Mosley's British Union of Fascists and the various parties in France – came close to power, although support for the latter did much to weaken French national unity as World War II approached.

Oswald Mosley (furthest right of the men wearing caps) inspects members of his British Union of Fascists in London's Royal Mint Street, October 1936.

Fascism also came to power in Spain in 1939, but only as a pale imitation of the German–Italian model. At this time most Spaniards were still either very rich or very poor, and there were no large middle or lower middle classes for the Spanish fascist party, the Falange, to recruit from. As a result, it was largely made up of enthusiastic students who lacked any political or military experience. When the **Spanish Civil War** broke out in 1936, the leaders of the army and the old upper class effectively took over the Falange – the army general Francisco Franco became its leader – and turned it into an organization which represented their interests. Franco welcomed help from Hitler and Mussolini, but refused to support them in World War II. He made no attempt to create a mass party or a totalitarian state on the German or Italian model, and pursued an unaggressive foreign policy. His fascism never demanded enthusiastic participation from his people, only obedience.

Fascism as a set of ideas and prejudices was fairly widespread in the world of the 1920s and 30s, and some of those ideas and prejudices lingered on after World War II in Franco's Spain and a few other countries. Fascism as a full-blooded system of political, social and economic organization only ever existed in Italy and Germany.

Japan

Japan was allied to Germany and Italy in World War II, but was never a fascist state in the fullest sense. In the 1930s the Japanese state shared some attributes with European fascism – an aggressive nationalism, glorification of the military and war, and a belief that the state was more important than the individual – but clearly lacked others. There was no one-party state, no inspiring individual leader.

Establishing dictatorships

Both Mussolini and Hitler came to power legally. Admittedly their supporters used violent intimidation during election campaigns, but their parties won a significant proportion of the national vote. They were invited to become heads of government by their respective heads of state, King Victor Emmanuel in Italy and President Hindenburg in Germany. For several years in Mussolini's case, and several months in Hitler's, they held office in political systems which were still supposedly **democratic**.

Of course, neither man had a democratic bone in his body. Neither had any intention of sharing power with anyone else if he could possibly help it. Both claimed that this was the way it should be. Democracy divided people, they said; their countries could only be united under one party, one man. Any who opposed that party, that man, were traitors to the whole nation. Such people needed imprisoning or killing, and the system had to be changed to make this possible.

Surrounded by other Nazi officials, Hitler's deputy Herman Goering opens a new road from Berlin to Stettin in April 1936.

From Prime Minister to *Duce*

FOR DETAILS ON KEY FASCISTS, SEE PAGES 59–60.

In 1924, when Mussolini had been in power for over a year, new elections were held in Italy. Before they took place, Mussolini changed the voting rules, so that the party with the largest number of votes – even if it was only 25 per cent of the total – got 66 per cent of the seats in the Italian **parliament**. With the help of widespread intimidation and other forms of cheating, the fascists managed to win the most votes.

There was still opposition, however. One well-known socialist MP named Giacomo Matteotti made an angry speech accusing Mussolini of rigging the elections. Soon after that he disappeared, and a few months later his body was found. There seems little doubt that Mussolini arranged the murder, but the outrage which followed the discovery of Matteotti's corpse seems to have unnerved him, and for several months he appeared unable to decide whether to enforce his authority or offer his resignation.

His mind was finally made up by a visit from Fascist Party colleagues. If he didn't get a grip on the country, they told him, then they would find someone else who would. A few days later Mussolini announced to parliament that he would become a dictator, in order to give Italy the peace and quiet he said it needed.

Over the next few years he took the necessary steps. Freedom of the press was ended in 1925. **Trade unions** and all political parties, except the Fascist Party, were banned in 1926, and discussion within the Fascist Party was effectively ended. The following year a political police force – the OVRA (Opera de Vigilanza e di Repressione dell'Anti-fascismo – the Force for Vigilance and Repression of Anti-fascism) was set up to seek out any illegal opposition.

17

By the end of the 1920s the only possible threats to Mussolini's authority came from the King, whose powers he had already managed to reduce, and the powerful Roman Catholic Church. He finally gained the Church's support for his dictatorship by paying it for land taken in the 19th century and giving it control over state education (the Lateran Treaty of 1929). Mussolini was now the undisputed leader, *il Duce*.

From Chancellor to *Führer*

In Germany the same process took much less time. When Hitler was appointed **Chancellor** in January 1933, he knew that he could be dismissed at any time by President Hindenburg, and there were only three other National Socialists in the cabinet. Fortunately for Hitler, one of these was his right-hand man Herman Goering, who as Prussian Minister of the Interior controlled two-thirds of Germany's local government and police, a source of potentially overwhelming power.

Hitler needed an excuse to use this power, and he soon found one. Elections had been called for 5 March, but on 27 February the **Reichstag** building was destroyed by fire. A Dutch **communist** named van der Lubbe was accused of setting it ablaze, but many now believe that the **Nazis** themselves were behind it. Hitler told Hindenburg that the fire had been the signal for a communist revolution, and turned the **SA** and Goering's police force loose. Thousands of communists and other potential enemies were arrested, beaten up or killed, and the elections on 5 March were held in an even more frightening atmosphere than usual.

Gun law

'With communist terrorism and raids there must be no trifling, and, when necessary, revolvers must be used without regard to the consequences. Police officers who fire their revolvers in execution of their duties will be protected by me without regard to the consequences of using their weapons. But officials who fail, out of mistaken regard for the consequences, to use their weapons must expect disciplinary action to be taken against them.'

(Hitler's deputy Herman Goering)

Smoke pours out of the burning Reichstag, 27 February 1933. The fire, which was probably set by the Nazis themselves, gave them the excuse they needed to imprison or murder communists.

The National Socialists still won only 43.9 per cent of the vote, but when parliament met on 23 March, SA troops prevented the communists from taking the 81 seats they had won with their 12 per cent of the vote. With the help of a few smaller **right-wing** parties, Hitler managed to get the 66 per cent majority he needed for the passing of an Enabling Act. This was a law which effectively allowed him to do whatever he wanted, without consulting parliament, for a period of four years. Within months, political parties and trade unions had been banned, local governments stripped of their powers, and the press and radio gagged. The **SS (Schutzstaffeln** – 'protection squad'), the black-shirted organization which had begun life as Hitler's personal bodyguard, was expanded into a force responsible for the political policing of the country.

The only possible opposition to Hitler now came from the German army and his own **paramilitary** organization, the brown-shirted SA. The SA's Ernst Röhm wanted to merge these two organizations under his leadership, but Hitler knew that such a move would both antagonize the army and give Röhm too much power. Getting rid of Röhm, however, would both reduce the threat to his own position and give the regular army cause to thank him. On 30 June 1934 Hitler took action. Röhm and many other SA leaders were murdered by the SS on what became known as the Night of the Long Knives.

A few weeks later President Hindenburg died, and Hitler announced that henceforth Germany would have only one leader, one *Führer* – himself.

In short ...

'The street gangs had seized control of the resources of a great modern state, the gutter had come to power.'

(English historian Alan Bullock)

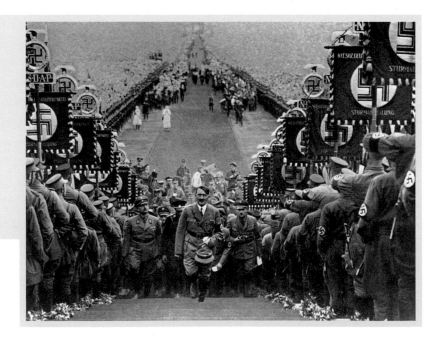

The *Führer* rises up through a sea of swastikas (the Nazi symbol) during a Nazi parade in Bückeburg, October 1934.

5 The fascist state

There was no forgetting who was the most important citizen of the fascist state. The leader, whether *Duce* or *Führer*, was never far away. Their pictures would appear on the front pages of newspapers, magazine covers and posters, their voices would pour out of radio sets and street loudspeakers. They were Nietzsche's imaginary 'supermen', made real, cleverer, braver and harder-working than any nation deserved. Their writings, like Hitler's *Mein Kampf*, were required reading. They were, as Italian slogans said of Mussolini, always right.

They took all the decisions that really mattered, and left their subordinates to squabble over those that didn't. The people as a whole were occasionally given the chance, in carefully arranged **plebiscites**, to express their satisfaction with the way things were going, but this illusion of taking part was all that remained of **democracy**. Rarely in modern history has such power been concentrated in individual hands.

Personality cult

'By 1926-27, the religion of *ducismo* [worship of Mussolini] was in full swing. School teachers were ordered to magnify this solitary figure, to stress his disinterestedness [lack of personal ambition], his wonderful courage and brilliant mind, and to teach that obedience to such a man was the highest virtue. His picture was already displayed on all public buildings and would sometimes be carried in procession through the streets like the image of a patron saint. Devout [strongly committed] fascists might have his photograph printed at the head of their writing paper ...'

(English historian Dennis Mack Smith)

The party

Below the level of the leader stood the party, the Fascist Party in Italy, the National Socialist Party in Germany. These parties played a crucial role in the **dictators**' rise to power, but once the dictatorships had been established, their function changed. They were no longer forums for discussion or organizations for winning elections, because the time for discussions and elections was over.

If Hitler and Mussolini had once represented the parties, now the parties represented Hitler and Mussolini. They were like huge overblown fan clubs.

Hitler, Goering and other Nazis take part in the annual Munich march to celebrate the 1923 uprising, November 1937.

All the key jobs in government, from national to local level, were held by party members. They conducted the day-to-day administration of the two countries for the two dictators, carrying out their economic and social policies, rounding up their latest enemies. They filled the stadiums and squares with their uniforms, marches, flaming torches and cries of devotion. Their party membership cards were badges of privilege and symbols of power.

The forces of law and order

Hitler never received a majority of votes in an election, and Mussolini's only electoral triumph was at least partly rigged. In both countries there were many who hated the fascists from the beginning, and many more who eventually grew disenchanted.

Opposition was easy to feel, but dangerous to express. In Germany each block of flats or group of houses had its resident National Socialist, ready to report on anyone who criticised the government or its leader, and the **SS** security service, the SD (Sicherheitsdienst), employed over 100,000 part-time **informers**. In Italy the OVRA also made people think twice about voicing their discontent. In both countries children were encouraged to report their parents for anti-fascist comments or behaviour.

Other reasons for obedience were provided by the new legal systems. Anyone accused of a political crime would appear before a Special Court in Germany, a Special Tribunal in Italy. There would be no jury, no independent judge, no right of appeal, no chance whatsoever of a fair trial. By the mid-1930s over 20,000 people had been imprisoned in the new German **concentration camps**. Italian prisons were less fearsome, and fewer people were imprisoned there.

Armies

The only other source of physical power within the fascist states were their armies. Both Mussolini and Hitler had been worried about the military at first, and with good reason. The Italian army had wanted to stop Mussolini's March on Rome, but had failed to persuade the King to give the order. Many of the German army's leaders despised Hitler as a lower-class upstart, and feared that he intended to replace them with the brown-shirted **SA**.

However, the army leaders were, on the whole, **right-wing** in their attitudes. They favoured **nationalist** ideas, and they were keen to see their forces expanded and better-equipped. Once the dictators had made it clear that their private armies offered no threat to the regular armies, and that the regular armies would be hugely expanded and placed once more at the centre of the national stage, most of the military leaders happily accepted fascism.

In later years the strain of defeat would destroy the relationship between dictators and army leaders in both countries, but there was little sign of friction in the 1930s. The two worked hand in hand to create the bigger and better military forces which both believed were in their interests.

Mussolini in characteristic pose – legs firmly planted, one arm raised, the other at his hip – speaking to troops in Rome.

6 The fascist economy

Fascism came to power in times of economic crises, and it was bound to be judged, at least in the beginning, by how successful it proved in dealing with those crises. Since both Mussolini's Fascist Party and Hitler's National Socialists had made great play of offering something to all classes of society, their solutions to their countries' economic problems had to seem fair to all those classes.

Mussolini was lucky in 1922. The economy was already beginning to grow when he took office, and he could spend the next few years happily taking credit for something which had nothing to do with him. However, there was no avoiding the **Great Depression**, which caused high unemployment in all the developed countries through the early 1930s, and seemed set to prove that the man who was always right was apparently sometimes wrong.

The Great Depression

In October 1929 a calamitous fall in share prices on the New York Stock Exchange – the Great Crash – triggered a worldwide economic slump, the Great Depression. Over the next few years, as world production and trade fell, unemployment rose dramatically. Germany, which relied on American loans to pay its way, was particularly badly hit. By January 1933, when Hitler came to power, around 40% of workers were without jobs.

In Germany the Great Depression was wonderful news for the National Socialists as long as they remained in opposition – their popularity soared as the country's misery deepened. Once in power, they too needed economic answers if they were to retain that popularity.

Spend, spend, spend

The solution which both the Italians and Germans hit on, more through luck than judgement, was to spend their way out of the depression. This, as the British economist John Maynard Keynes had been arguing, was the correct response. Spending money on things that needed doing – on anything from picking up leaves to building river dams – stimulated economies back into growth.

Hitler's car about to break the ribbon on the first of the new *Autobahns* – motorways from Frankfurt to Darmstadt.

This was great news for Hitler and Mussolini, who were already keen to spend money on things they thought their nations needed. These included schools, hospitals, impressive public buildings, streamlined trains and new motorways. Fascism liked to think of itself as the most modern of **ideologies**.

Motorways, of course, had other important uses. They made it easier to transport large numbers of motorized troops and tanks, and they served as emergency landing strips for military aircraft. Hitler began rebuilding the German armed forces the moment he took office, and this vast programme of **rearmament** was the **Nazi** government's single biggest item of spending. Germany, and to a much lesser extent Italy, bought its way out of the Great Depression by preparing for war.

Working conditions

For the ordinary people of the two countries, things soon looked a lot better than they had at the height of the Depression. Unemployment fell swiftly, and almost everyone benefited. The lower and middle classes had better job security and could take heart from the fact that the gap between rich and poor was narrowing. The rich businessmen who had supported fascism were still rich, and no longer had to worry about labour problems. Everyone could take pride in the fact that the nation was on the move once again.

In Italy Mussolini divided industry up into 22 giant corporations, which he said would be run jointly by owners, managers and workers. In reality it was the owners and the Fascist Party who took all the important decisions. Like so much else in Mussolini's world, the corporations were essentially a cheat.

The 'Flying Duce', a new Italian streamlined train which was capable of travelling over 100 miles an hour in 1938.

The two regimes never tired of emphasizing the positive features of their economic policies. They were understandably reluctant to point out the negative features. Wages were kept low, and hours were frequently long. It was always difficult, and often impossible, to move from job to job. Once the **trade unions** had been abolished there was no way for workers to press for improvements in their working conditions.

The need for war

The German economy actually looked in much better shape than it really was. It was building motorways and tanks, but Germany could not sell motorways and its leader wanted the tanks for his own use. There was not enough real money coming in, and the government was printing more and more banknotes to disguise that fact. At some point in the not-too-distant future it would have to find new sources of income.

The government could of course raise taxes, but this would involve hardship for a large number of Germans, and would cost the National Socialists their popularity. Hitler preferred to seek out new sources of income beyond Germany's borders, to solve Germany's economic problems by forcibly seizing the wealth of others through conquest.

7 The totalitarian society

The fascist states were not simply **dictatorships**. They were dictatorships which demanded the whole-hearted commitment of all their people. Mussolini and Hitler were the model for citizens to follow. Their way of looking at things was the only correct way of looking at things, and enormous effort was put into making sure that the people knew, understood and actively shared their leaders' views in all matters that could remotely be considered political. This sort of society, which allows no opposition and no other points of view, is usually called **totalitarian**.

The news media and the arts

The news **media** were strictly controlled by the governments; both newspapers and radio put out a steady stream of fascist **propaganda**. Those caught listening to foreign radio stations risked ending up in a **concentration camp**. Under Hitler and Mussolini it was almost impossible for most Germans or Italians to get an accurate picture of what was really happening in their countries.

The arts – literature, painting, film – were also held in a rigid fascist embrace. Both Hitler and Mussolini liked to think of themselves as artists – Mussolini played the violin, Hitler painted – but neither allowed any freedom of artistic expression.

Nazis and their supporters feeding a bonfire with what they considered 'anti-German literature' in Berlin, May 1933.

In Germany in particular, anything which even faintly suggested opposition to fascism or its regime was forbidden, banned or destroyed. There were public bonfires for books which were considered dangerous, and many of the country's most famous artists moved abroad.

Those artists who flourished either worked in non-political areas or were involved in producing propaganda for the regime. The film-maker Leni Riefenstahl was a good example of the latter, and her film *Triumph of the Will*, which glorified physical strength and other racial characteristics considered uniquely German, was perhaps **Nazi** Germany's most memorable piece of art. In most respects fascism proved a cultural wasteland.

German film director Leni Riefenstahl stands next to a large stone eagle at a stadium in Nuremberg, during her filming of *Triumph of the Will* in 1934.

The modern dictator

'Hitler's dictatorship differed in one fundamental point from all its predecessors in history. His was the first dictatorship ... which made complete use of all technical means for the domination of its own country. Through technical devices like the radio and the loudspeaker, 80 million people were deprived of independent thought. It was thereby possible to subject them to the will of one man .... '

(Nazi leader Albert Speer, speaking at the Nuremberg Trials after World War II)

Women and children

Both regimes placed great importance on indoctrinating children (filling their heads) with fascist ideas. The only general textbook in Italy's elementary schools, the *Libro Unico*, was crammed full of praise for fascism and the man who created it. All German teachers were required to join the National Socialist Teachers' League, and to swear an oath that they would be loyal and obedient to Adolf Hitler. Their handbook described Hitler's book *Mein Kampf* as 'our infallible guiding star'.

Members of the Italian youth movement, the Balilla, waiting outside Rome railway station to greet the visiting British Prime Minister, Neville Chamberlain, in January 1939.

31

Particularly in Germany, information of all kinds was twisted to fit the fascist party line, sometimes to an almost laughable extent (though the consequences were far from laughable). Albert Einstein was a great physicist, but because he was a Jew, German physics students had to do without his groundbreaking **Theory of Relativity**. In their history lessons they were told that the German army had not really lost World War I, but had been stabbed in the back by liberals, socialists and Jews.

Outside school, there was no relief. From around the age of six, children in both Italy and Germany were expected to join youth organizations. The main organizations for teenage boys were the Italian **Balilla** and German **Hitlerjugend** (Hitler Youth), both of which featured smart uniforms, rifle drill and weapons training, long hikes and organized sports, and more doses of fascist indoctrination.

The girls had their own groups, but none of the military training. On the contrary, they were taught that their future place was in the home, preferably with lots of children. The fascists liked to think of themselves as modern thinkers, but their attitudes to women were utterly **reactionary**. Women were actively discouraged from working or wearing make-up, and were offered medals for bearing large numbers of children. 'War is to the male what childbearing is to the female' was one of Mussolini's favourite slogans. *Kinde, Kirche, Küche* was the German recipe for women – children, church, kitchen. It might not be what they wanted, but it was what the state required. Between 1931 and 1937 the number of women attending university in Germany fell by 50 per cent.

Leisure

Without **trade union** representation and the freedom to change jobs, adults were increasingly controlled during working hours. Like the children, they were expected to dedicate their time to fascism at the end of the working day. Organizations like the Italian Dopolavoro (After Work) and the German Kraft durch Freude (Strength through Joy) did their best to fill up people's leisure time.

Cheap tickets were handed out for pro-fascist plays and films, but the greatest efforts were put into arranging sports contests and physically demanding holidays of all descriptions. These outdoor activities were supposed to make the nation fitter, both for fighting and for bearing children. They were also supposed to make everyone feel part of the whole – happy cogs in the huge fascist machine. In Franco's Spain someone who kept to himself was ignored; in Italy, and even more in Germany, such a person was considered anti-social, an insult to the regime.

Acceptance is not enough

'It is not enough to reconcile people to [get them to accept] our regime, to move them towards a position of neutrality towards us. We want rather to work on people until they are addicted to us.'

(Hitler's propaganda minister Joseph Goebbels)

FOR DETAILS ON KEY FASCISTS, SEE PAGES 59–60.

DER DEUTSCHE STUDENT

Propaganda for the Nazi ideal: a smiling blond and blue-eyed student proudly holds the Nazi flag.

Religion

Before the fascist takeovers, many Italians and Germans had been active church-goers, mostly Catholics in Italy, both Protestants and Catholics in Germany. Neither Mussolini nor Hitler was religious, and both looked down on the Churches, but they knew better than to risk an all-out assault. Mussolini actually did a deal with the powerful Roman Catholic Church in Italy, allowing it to supervise education in return for blessing his regime.

In Germany, Hitler chose to ignore the Churches. Only a few brave churchmen and women dared stand up to him, and he probably hoped that a constant diet of fascist propaganda would eventually turn people away from Christianity, which he considered a religion fit only for slaves.

Fascism's outcasts

Finally, there were some who could never be part of the whole, who by their very nature were excluded from participation in fascism's – and particularly German fascism's – celebration of the model fascist citizen. This model citizen was of Aryan stock (non-Jewish German), heterosexual, strong in mind and body. Anyone who failed to fit this bill was liable to persecution and worse.

Gay people were persecuted from the beginning, and frequently ended up in concentration camps. The mentally disabled fared just as badly – on the outbreak of the war Hitler ordered the 'mercy' killing of some 100,000 so-called incurables. Such crimes were almost beyond belief, but even they were eclipsed by the fate which awaited the so-called non-Aryan races – the Jews and the **gypsies**.

8 Fascism and racism

When things go wrong one frequent reaction is to look for someone to blame. This is true of both individuals and societies. Sometimes the person or group chosen to bear the blame for whatever it is that has gone wrong is completely blameless. Such persons or groups are called **scapegoats**.

By its very nature, fascism had more need for scapegoats than other political systems. It claimed that it had a cure for the problems of each and every social class, that it could magic away the conflict of interests between rich and poor and create a truly unified nation. This was impossible. In reality, fascism could only create unity by stressing a common national identity and inventing common enemies, enemies which all the nation could share. Outside the nation's borders these could be other nations, but inside the borders such enemies had to be defined along political or racial lines. Fascism was not, in the beginning, a **racist ideology**, but in practice it was likely to become so.

Why Nazi Germany was racist
In Italy, Mussolini remained reasonably popular right up to the mid-1930s, and there was little need of an internal scapegoat. In Germany, however, several factors combined to make scapegoats of the country's Jewish population.

Nazi stormtroopers hold up placards which say: 'Germans! Defend yourselves! Don't buy from Jews!', April 1933.

Over the previous 100 years the notion of German racial superiority, and the subsequent importance of maintaining the purity of the supposed Aryan (non-Jewish German) master-race, had been put forward by several influential **philosophers**. When Hitler came to power, the Jews formed about 1 per cent of the German population of some 60 million. They were the only internal threat to this strange notion of racial purity.

The Jews were a large enough minority to be noticeable, small enough to be virtually powerless. They were thought of as money-makers – 17 per cent of German bankers in 1925 were Jews. This made them a potential target for the poor. A high proportion of well-known **communists** were Jews, which made them a potential target for the rich. Jews also occupied prominent positions in professions like medicine and teaching, which created much envy among the middle classes, particularly in times of hardship. As a group they offered the **Nazis** an almost perfect scapegoat.

Hitler's personal hatred of the Jews – he had been blaming them for his and the world's failures since his youth – added yet another reason for attacking them. His blind prejudice, justified to himself by an absurd belief in racial purity, was given added weight by the usefulness of having someone to blame for all of Germany's ills. It turned German fascism into a system which soon became notorious for its racism.

Campaign of persecution

The **persecution** of the German Jews began slowly but soon gathered momentum. A **boycott** of Jewish businesses was followed by the Nuremberg Laws, issued in September 1935. These stripped German Jews of their German citizenship, forbade marriages between Jews and Germans, and prohibited Jews from employing German servants at a time when such employment was commonplace.

By 1936 more than half the Jews in Germany were prevented from working by either new laws or intimidation. All over the country signs went up forbidding Jews from sharing previously common facilities. 'Bathing prohibited for dogs and Jews' was one such instruction at a swimming lake. At the same time, every effort was made to stamp out Jewish influence in the arts and sciences. The new atomic physics – 'Jewish physics' – was ridiculed, and many Jewish writers, artists and entertainers moved abroad. Jews in general were encouraged to consider emigration (moving abroad to live), though only on condition that they left their money and valuables behind.

This campaign of persecution reached a climax on 9 November 1938. Ernst vom Rath, a German politician in Paris, was murdered by a Jew and this was used as the excuse for a night of violent retribution. All across Germany, officially organized mobs attacked Jewish homes and businesses, murdering over 90 people. It was called Kristallnacht (Crystal Night) because of all the broken glass which littered the streets. Many German Jews who had continued to hope that the Nazis would outgrow their **anti-Semitism** now decided to join the wave of emigration.

The aftermath of Kristallnacht, when the Nazis organized attacks against the Jewish community in Germany.

Kristallnacht

'One friend from a town in northern Germany told me that the Nazis there made a huge fire with books and other things, and made the Jewish families stand all around the fire. Behind the families stood the Nazis with their bayonets [blades attached to their rifles] drawn. To go forward was the fire, to go back, the bayonets. The Jews stood there and were forced to cry, "We are the murderers! We are the murderers!"'

(German Jew Martha Pappenheim, describing one of the many atrocities which took place on 9–10 November 1938, from an unpublished manuscript)

By this time, Mussolini had climbed aboard the anti-Semitic bandwagon. He seems to have had no deep personal hatred of the Jews, but he was keen to please Hitler. He had also begun to realize, as his regime lost popularity in the second half of the 1930s, that the Jews might prove a useful scapegoat for his own failures. Anti-Semitic laws were eventually introduced, but most Italians disapproved of them, and they were not enforced as rigorously in Italy as they were in Germany.

The obscene climax

When war broke out in September 1939 emigration was no longer an option for Germany's Jews, and as the area conquered by the German armed forces increased over the next few years, millions more Jews found themselves at the Nazis' mercy. As the German army drove towards Moscow through the summer and autumn of 1941, it was followed by **SS** units called Einsatzgruppen (task forces), whose sole purpose was to murder Jews and communist officials. Some 600,000 were murdered in six months, shot after being forced to dig their own graves.

Early in 1942, at the Wannsee Conference, the German fascist regime decided to implement what it called the final solution to the Jewish problem: the organized murder of all those Jews now living in German-controlled areas. Extermination camps, like Auschwitz in German-occupied Poland, were created with the facilities needed to gas thousands of people to death each day. They received trainloads of victims from all over Europe, and by the end of the war some six million Jews – and around half a million gypsies – had perished at the hands of the German fascists and their foreign helpers. German fascism had turned racism into **genocide**.

Hundreds of corpses at a German concentration camp, awaiting burial at the end of World War II.

Roads to war

Think of fascism – Italian, German or any other kind – and the images which come to mind are of leaders in uniform shaking their fists, of uniformed men filling streets or invading someone else's country, of violence and its victims. Fascism and war seemed made for each other.

Born in war

Fascism came out of a war, World War I. It took root in the frustration and bitterness of those Italians and Germans who believed that their suffering and sacrifices had been in vain. Most of its early supporters, and both its leaders, were soldiers. Hitler never tired of telling people that he had once been an ordinary soldier amongst the masses. Mussolini described the explosion in February 1917 which riddled him with metal fragments as 'the most beautiful moment of my life'. Both men were happier in uniform than civilian clothes, both delighted in drama, display and the pure physical force of military parades. The first fascists were Mussolini's fighting groups, and the use of force was central to their political beliefs. War was more than a way of getting what the nation wanted, it was the nation's chance to find and display its true fascist self.

Fascism was intensely **nationalistic**. According to their own **propaganda**, the Germans were a master race held down by all the lesser nations which surrounded them. According to Mussolini, Italians had already created the greatest empire in history – the Roman Empire – and were now ready to rebuild it. Neither leader made any secret of the fact that the current international arrangements stood in their way. Their nationalism had to be aggressive.

Foreign scapegoats

Fascism needed **scapegoats**. Who was holding Italy and Germany back? At home there were **socialists** and Jews, and abroad there were those nations which occupied Italy's and Germany's rightful place.

The British and the French had conquered half the world, the fascists claimed, but they refused to allow anyone else to share in their good fortune. It was the duty of the fascist nations to fight back against this oppression in every way they could. Furthermore, military adventures would take people's mind off their hardships at home, and military successes would boost people's faith in fascism and their leaders.

Fascism was **dictatorial** and **totalitarian**. It did its best to convince its citizens that war was a truly noble endeavour. A tightly controlled media delivered the regime's arguments for aggressive behaviour and no arguments for any other course of action. Many, particularly in Germany, were willing to accept such arguments. Those who disagreed had no way of saying so without putting their lives, and the lives of their families, at risk.

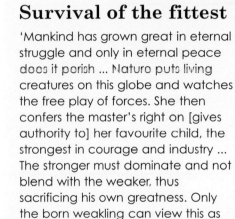

Survival of the fittest

'Mankind has grown great in eternal struggle and only in eternal peace does it perish ... Nature puts living creatures on this globe and watches the free play of forces. She then confers the master's right on [gives authority to] her favourite child, the strongest in courage and industry ... The stronger must dominate and not blend with the weaker, thus sacrificing his own greatness. Only the born weakling can view this as cruel ...'

(Adolf Hitler, explaining in *Mein Kampf* that domination by the strong is both inevitable and right)

Finally, German fascism was a system built for war. The **rearmament** programme which helped to pull Germany out of the **Great Depression** had, by 1936, begun to act as a drag on the economy. Someone had to pay for it. Hitler was left with the choice of either slowing his rearmament programme and effectively giving up hope of overtaking the other great powers, or of accelerating the programme and relying on the spoils of future expansion to pay for it. His nature was aggressive, and so was fascism. It is not surprising that he chose a policy of expansion.

Abyssinia

There was always one good reason for not being aggressive – the fear of defeat and humiliation. Mussolini began his leadership with two minor successes in 1923. He forced Greece to pay compensation for a murdered Italian tourist and persuaded Yugoslavia to give up the disputed town of Fiume. After that, he adopted a very cautious approach. He talked a lot about the glories of war but did nothing to involve himself in one.

This peaceful period ended in 1935. Encouraged by the emergence of **Nazi** Germany, and eager to take his people's mind off their economic troubles at home, he finally took the plunge and ordered the invasion of Abyssinia, the only independent state in Africa. Britain and France objected, and the **League of Nations** introduced some half-hearted

Italian troops on the march during the invasion of Abyssinia in 1935. Most of the killing was done from the air.

economic sanctions, but by 1936 the Italian army had completed its conquest, thanks in part to its use of poison gas. Fascism had triumphed, and Mussolini's popularity reached new heights. Bullying seemed to work.

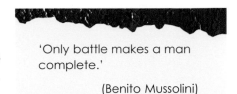

'Only battle makes a man complete.'

(Benito Mussolini)

From the Rhineland to Poland

This message was not lost on Hitler. The aims of his foreign policy, as outlined in *Mein Kampf*, were to recover the lands that Germany had lost in 1918 and conquer additional *lebensraum* (living space) for the German people in Eastern Europe. His first risky move – the first occasion on which he gave the British and French a good excuse to use force against him – was the military reoccupation of the **Rhineland** in March 1936 (the **Treaty of Versailles** had forbidden Germany from stationing troops in this part of their country). The British and French did nothing.

Hitler now turned his attention to countries containing significant German communities. Some regions, like French Alsace, Silesia and Danzig in Poland, had been part of Germany until 1918. Others, like Austria and the Sudetenland area of Czechoslovakia, had been part of the old **Austro-Hungarian Empire**. The Treaty of Versailles had scattered all these Germans, but it had also come out in favour of the principle of self-determination, the right of peoples to rule themselves. Hitler played on this, claiming that all he wanted was self-determination for Germans, and that once he got it he would be content.

Hoping against hope that he was speaking the truth, or simply hoping that he would turn east against the Soviet Union, the Western powers made no real effort to stop him when he swallowed up Austria in March 1938, and actually

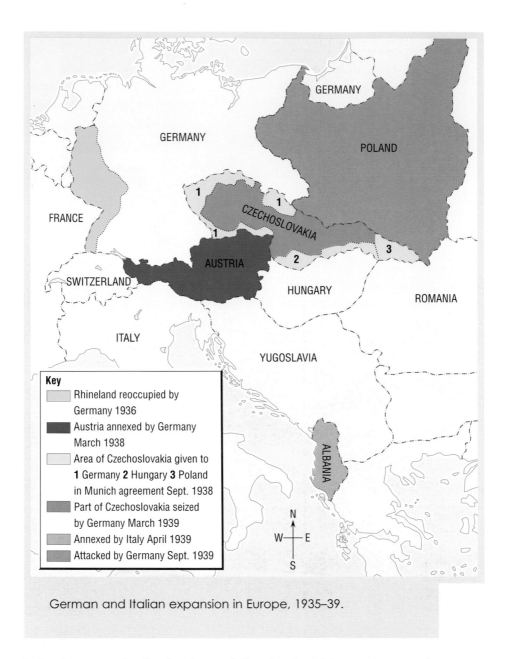

German and Italian expansion in Europe, 1935–39.

helped persuade the leaders of Czechoslovakia to give up the
Sudetenland at the Munich Conference that September. It was
only in March 1939, when Hitler ordered the invasion and
occupation of the rest of Czechoslovakia – which had no German
population – that the Western powers awoke from their trance
and pledged to fight if he moved against Poland.

With friends like this ...

Mussolini followed this last German move by invading Albania, but the two leaders were not following any grand fascist plan. There was no Fascist International along the lines of the **Communist International**, little discussion of how the two countries' military machines might co-operate with each other, and nothing remotely like a joint plan of action. Hitler did not think he needed any help from Italy, and Mussolini's only real worry was that he might miss out on any available booty.

Hitler and Mussolini looking pleased with themselves during the German leader's visit to Florence, May 1938. The war which would destroy them both was still 15 months away.

⑩ Fascism at war

Germany started World War II by invading Poland on 1 September 1939. Two years of almost unbroken military success followed. Poland was conquered with ease, Norway and Denmark occupied, the British and French armies in France broken apart by a lightning campaign. The British, though victorious in the Battle of Britain, were left on the defensive, and Hitler felt able to turn his armies east, against the Soviet Union. By September 1941 they were more than halfway to Moscow and apparent victory.

Early successes

The German fascists had inherited a long tradition of German military excellence. The army, in particular, had brilliant strategists, wonderful organization and a democratic spirit which was completely at odds with the political masters it served. Hitler and his movement deserved at least some of the credit for the stunning run of success in 1939–41.

Hitler and his deputy Hermann Goering discussing matters of state.

The fascist obsession with outdoor activities created fit and well-trained soldiers, and Hitler showed himself willing and able to build on the armed forces' existing qualities. He was quick to understand the potential of modern weapons like tanks. Unlike most of his generals, he grasped the brilliance of a daring plan for an attack on France, and forced the the generals to implement it, with astonishing success. In the summer of 1940, with France beaten and Britain locked out of Europe, fascism's future looked rosy.

Fatal flaws

From this point on, however, those aspects of fascism which hampered its successful conduct of a war became more and more evident. The next crucial decision was taken by Mussolini. He had brought Italy into the war only days before the French surrender, and felt he deserved some glory of his own. That autumn he decided to attack Greece from newly occupied Albania. This was a bad decision, but in fascist Italy there was no one willing or able to argue Mussolini out of it.

Hitler was not given the chance to do so. He had never given Mussolini any advance warning of German actions, so Mussolini decided not to warn Hitler of this Italian attack. 'He will find out from the papers that I have occupied Greece,' Mussolini said. He was much more interested in scoring points against his fellow dictator than in real co-operation.

Nor was Italy ready for this or any other war. Mussolini had been telling his generals to prepare for war for almost 20 years, but had completely failed to provide them with the tools they needed. In the end he came to believe his own fascist propaganda and all those subordinates who told him what he wanted to hear. A system in which all power was concentrated in the hands of one man who rarely heard the truth was unlikely to be efficient. The Italian troops sent to fight in Greece's snowbound mountains were badly armed and badly supplied. Their shoes were made of cardboard.

More of the same

Not surprisingly, the attack on Greece proved a disaster.
The furious Germans were forced to intervene, and their
planned attack on the Soviet Union was put back by
several crucial weeks. At first this did not seem to matter,
but as the Russian campaign ran on into the autumn and
winter of 1941 the military defects of fascism began to
show through. Hitler, like Mussolini, had never been one
to take advice, and his successes in 1940 had made him
even less inclined to listen to his generals. When he began
to make mistakes – like his decision in late 1942 to take
and hold the Russian city of Stalingrad – no one had the
power or influence to argue him out of them.

Red Army troops advance through the rubble during the battle of
Stalingrad. This battle, which lasted for six months and involved
over half a million men, was probably the most decisive
engagement of World War II.

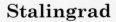

Stalingrad

Stalingrad was originally one of the less important targets of the German army's Russian offensive in the summer of 1942. However, stiff Russian resistance and the name of the city – literally, 'Stalin's town' – persuaded Hitler that its capture was more important than it really was. He ended up committing over a quarter of a million men to a street-by-street struggle which lasted several months, and which ended with the German troops surrounded and forced to surrender.

It was also becoming apparent by this time that Germany was far from ready to fight a global war. Hitler and his generals had created a *blitzkrieg* ('lightning war') force of tanks and planes which could take on any enemy over a small area and a limited period of time, but they had not prepared for the war they were now having to fight. There had been no barges ready for an invasion of Britain in June 1940, there were not enough U-boats (*Unterseeboots* – submarines) to fight the Battle of the Atlantic, and there were not enough soldiers to conquer and hold the vast expanses of Russia.

More important still, there was no one to sort out the mess. As in Italy, those in charge of different parts of the war machine all reported to the leader, who played them off against each other. There was no attempt to impose any overall organization, as was the case in Britain, America and the Soviet Union.

The **reactionary** attitude towards women also played a part. While the women of Britain, Ameria and the Soviet Union worked in weapons factories, the women of Germany stayed at home. The work in German armament factories was done, with little efficiency, by foreign workers and prisoners, neither of whom had any interest in weapons that worked well.

Prisoners working in the tailor's workshop at Sachsenhausen **concentration camp**, February 1941.

The final nail

Finally, and perhaps most importantly of all, fascism's **racism** and extreme **nationalism** created enemies faster than its war machines could destroy them. When the Germans invaded the Soviet Union in 1941 many were prepared to welcome them as liberators from Stalin's rule, but these would-be allies soon changed their minds. **Tyranny**, after all, was all that the German **Nazis** and Italian Fascists offered to the people they conquered, and tyranny provokes people to fight back.

Yugoslavia, for example, was conquered in days by German tank columns, but the country was never really secured.

Resistance groups sprang up, and for the next three years large forces of German infantry fought unsuccessfully to contain them. The same pattern was repeated right across occupied Europe.

From early 1943 the fascist armies were in retreat. That summer Mussolini was voted out of office by his own subordinates and then arrested by the King of Italy. Rescued by a German airborne unit, he carried on the war from northern Italy, but it was now only a matter of time for both him and Hitler. Through 1944 the German armies retreated westward across Russia, up the Italian peninsula, and, finally, eastward across France. Late in April 1945 Mussolini was caught and shot by Italian **partisans**; a few days later Hitler took his own life rather than surrender to the Soviet conquerors of Berlin.

Their brutal ambition had laid waste a continent and cost 30 million men, women and children their lives. Fascism, as a serious approach to social and political organization, died with them.

11 So, what is fascism?

In the years since fascism's defeat in World War II, the words 'fascist' and 'fascism' have been used with less and less precision, and have become little more than words of abuse for anything considered too far to the political **right**. Fascism, with its heavy emphasis on **nationalism** and its tolerance towards big business, was certainly a movement of the right, but not all movements of the right were or are fascist. A strong preference for individual freedom over the interests of the community as a whole is also associated with the right, but few regimes have offered their citizens less personal freedom, or claimed more stridently to represent the collective interest, than **Nazi** Germany or fascist Italy.

Rise and fall

So, what exactly is fascism? As a system of political, social and economic organization it has, to date, only been adopted in Italy (1922–43) and Germany (1933–45), although a much diluted version did exist in Spain for over 30 years. As a set of ideas and prejudices (opinions formed beforehand), it won a large number of followers, but not power, in many other countries between the wars. Since World War II, true fascism has won so few followers as to be virtually insignificant.

Nazi leaders on trial for war crimes at Nuremberg in 1946. Hitler's deputy Hermann Goering, his head turned away from the camera, sits at the left-hand end of the dock's front row.

Fascism emerged in the aftermath of the World War I as an angry response to the problems of economic depression and supposed national humiliation. In both Italy and Germany, highly persuasive leaders promised order and an essentially false national unity to societies which seemed to be coming apart at the seams.

Once in power, both leaders – Mussolini slowly, Hitler at great speed – moved to destroy any potential opposition to their personal rule, both inside their own parties and in their societies as a whole. Their **dictatorships** were more than political. They expected their fascist ideas to guide people's whole lives. Adults and children, whether at work or leisure, were subject to an unending barrage of **propaganda** and kept in line by huge spy networks. Those who would not or could not fit in – **communists**, homosexuals, the mentally ill and physically handicapped, other races – were subject to increasingly murderous **persecution**, particularly in Germany.

Fascist success in overcoming the **Great Depression** was based on public works and **rearmament** programmes, but these could not be continued indefinitely without destroying the countries' ability to compete in the international market. By 1936–37 the choice for Germany lay between accepting that things would have to get worse before they could get better and seeking to balance the books through taking over other countries. Hitler's ambition and fascism's natural aggressiveness made war inevitable.

Fascism's natural defects played a crucial role in determining the outcome of World War II. Fascist dictatorships were economically inefficient, over-reliant on their flawed dictators, and incapable of winning whole-hearted support or even neutral acceptance from other nations or races. Fascism, in fact, was a born loser.

Post-war echoes

During the period between the wars, parties in other countries imitated Italian and German fascism, and during the war some of them saw a brief period of power as **puppet rulers**.

FOR DETAILS ON KEY FASCISTS, SEE PAGES 59–60.

Only Franco's regime in Spain survived the war, and by the 1950s Spanish fascism was little more than a dictatorship for preserving the economic privileges of the upper classes. Spain under Franco was a police state which allowed no political opposition, but it was never a **totalitarian state** like Mussolini's Italy or Hitler's Germany.

The Argentinian regime of Juan Perón and his wife Evita in the late 1940s and 1950s has sometimes been described as fascist. Here there was a genuine popular movement, a mass party, and persuasive leaders who offered an appeal to national unity which was essentially unreal. But the Peróns never established a complete dictatorship, let alone a totalitarian state.

A passing horror

'Fascism dissolved like a clump of earth thrown into a river ... disappeared with the world crisis that had allowed it to emerge.'

(English historian Eric Hobsbawm)

Many world leaders in the last half-century have been persuasive, many have been brutal, and many have used racial minorities as **scapegoats** to build popularity or cover up their failures. But the peculiar circumstances which gave rise to fascism between the wars have not appeared again. Those parties, particularly in Europe, which are most closely associated with fascism in the public mind – the British National Party in England and the Front National in France, for example – are more **racist** than fascist. Whether their scapegoating of racial minorities will prove politically successful in any future economic depression remains an open question.

54

An optimist might hope that humanity has learned its lesson once and for all. Fascism, briefly and misleadingly, led a substantial portion of two peoples to believe that it could solve the economic and social problems which afflicted their societies. It could not. It tried to cloak its failure in lies, violence and war, but war finally revealed it for the empty brutality it was. Most political **philosophies** have offered the human race at least something that was worth believing in. Fascism offered nothing.

The National Front Party in Britain, in a march against refugees and immigration in April 2001.

55

Timeline

1883	Benito Mussolini is born in Romagna, Italy
1889	Adolf Hitler is born in Braunau, Austria
1914	World War I; Hitler joins the German army
1915	Italy joins the war; Mussolini is called up
1917	Mussolini, badly wounded, is invalided out of the army
	Communist revolution in Russia
1918	Hitler wins his second Iron Cross for bravery
	World War I ends with German defeat
1919	Mussolini founds the Fasci di Combattimento in Milan
	Treaty of Versailles takes territory from Germany and imposes reparations
	Hitler joins the German Workers' Party (later the National Socialist Party)
1920–22	Reign of terror by Mussolini's armed gangs
1921	Hitler becomes leader of National Socialist (**Nazi**) Party. Forms the **SA**.
1922	The March on Rome leads to Mussolini's appointment as Prime Minister
1923	Hitler tries to seize power in Munich, but is arrested
1924	Hitler is sent to prison; writes *Mein Kampf*; is released the same year
	Murder of Matteotti in Italy
1924–27	Mussolini dismantles Italy's **democratic** system
1925	**SS** formed
1925–29	Period of prosperity helps Mussolini's popularity but weakens Nazis
1927	Legion of the Archangel Michael founded in Romania
1929	Great Crash on New York Stock Exchange triggers the **Great Depression**
1930	Extreme economic hardship in Germany sees rise in Nazi fortunes
1932	Nazis become largest single party in **Reichstag**
	Oswald Mosley founds the British Union of Fascists
1933	Hitler is appointed **Chancellor**, begins to dismantle German democratic system
	José Antonio Primo de Rivera founds the Falange in Spain

1934	Hitler destroys opposition inside Nazi party on Night of the Long Knives
	First meeting between Mussolini and Hitler
1935	Nuremberg Laws against the Jews introduced
	Mussolini orders the invasion of Abyssinia
1936	Italy's armed forces conquer Abyssinia
	Hitler orders remilitarization of the **Rhineland**
	The **Spanish Civil War** begins
	Hitler and Mussolini agree treaty of alliance, the Rome–Berlin Axis
1938	Hitler takes over Austria (the *Anschluss* – union)
	The Munich Conference awards the Czech Sudetenland to Germany
1939	Hitler takes over the rest of Czechoslovakia
	Mussolini successfully invades Albania
	Hitler signs Nazi–Soviet pact with Stalin
	German invasion of Poland begins World War II
1940	German defeat of France
	Mussolini brings Italy into the war on Germany's side
	Germany loses the Battle of Britain
1941	Italy unsuccessfully invades Greece
	German invasion of Soviet Union
	German armies halted outside Moscow and Leningrad
1942	Wannsee Conference decides on extermination of Jews
	Catastrophic German defeats at Stalingrad and El Alamein
1943	British and Americans invade Italy; Mussolini forced from power
	Mussolini rescued by German paratroopers
1944	German retreat on all fronts
1945	Fascism defeated. Mussolini killed by **partisans**, Hitler commits suicide.
1946	Surviving members of Nazi regime put on trial at Nuremberg

Further reading

Peter Chrisp, *The Rise of Fascism* (Wayland, 1991)

David Downing, *Benito Mussolini* (Heinemann Library, 2001)

Ilse Koehn, *Mischling, Second Degree* (Penguin, 1997)

Hugh Purcell, *Fascism* (Hamish Hamilton, 1977)

Morton Rhue, *The Wave* (Puffin Plus, 1994)

Richard Tames, *Fascism* (Hodder Wayland, 2000)

David Taylor, *Adolf Hitler* (Heinemann Library, 2001)

Sources

Alan Bullock, *Hitler: A Study in Tyranny* (Pelican, 1962)

Eric Hobsbawm, *Age of Extremes* (Penguin, 1994)

Ian Kershaw, *Hitler* (2 vols) (Allen Lane, 1998/2000)

Martin Kitchen, *Fascism* (Macmillan, 1976)

Dennis Mack Smith, *Mussolini* (Weidenfeld and Nicholson, 1981)

Films and plays

Schindler's List (film directed by Stephen Spielberg)

Triumph of the Will (film directed by Leni Riefenstahl)

Chicken Soup with Barley (play written by Arnold Wesker)

Websites

University of Wisconsin-Madison website on the history of fascism
in Italy:

www.library.wisc.edu/libraries/dpf/Fascism/Home.html

Encarta article – Fascism:

encarta.msn.com/index/conciseindex/41/04196000.htm?
z=1&pg=2&br=1

BBC education – Rise in fascism:

www.bbc.co.uk/education/modern/fascism/fascihtm.htm

BBC education – Nazi Germany:

www.bbc.co.uk/education/modern/nazi/nazihtm.htm

History Place – Hitler Youth:

www.historyplace.com/worldwar2/hitleryouth/index.html

School History web site – Weimar & Nazi Germany:

www.schoolshistory.org.uk/weimar.htm

Key fascists

Francisco Franco (1892–1975) was a leader of the army revolt which eventually overthrew the Spanish Republic in the **Spanish Civil War**. In 1937 he took over leadership of Spain's fascist party, the Falange, and during the civil war he welcomed support from both Germany and Italy. Franco was more of a **reactionary** than a true fascist, and he refused to join Germany and Italy in World War II. After that war his anti-**communism** and military usefulness brought support from the USA. It was not until his death that Spain began to emerge from the backwardness to which his dictatorship had condemned it.

Joseph Goebbels (1897–1945) became Hitler's Minister of **Propaganda** in 1933. He was responsible for controlling radio, the press and all other sources of information and opinion in the interests of the **Nazi** regime. Like Hitler, he was a persuasive speaker. He stayed with his leader to the last, committing suicide with his wife and six children in the *Führerbunker* (Hitler's underground headquarters) during the final days of the war.

Hermann Goering (1893–1946) was a famous fighter pilot in World War I. He joined the National Socialists in 1922 and soon became one of Hitler's right-hand men. As Minister of State for Prussia in the early years of Hitler's rule, he played a vital role in the destruction of **democracy** and the establishment of the Nazi **dictatorship**. His jobs included running the Gestapo security police until 1936, and the German economy from then until 1943. Sentenced to death at Nuremberg after the war, he committed suicide in his prison cell.

Heinrich Himmler (1900–45) was one of Hitler's closest colleagues. He was head of the **SS**, which began life as Hitler's personal bodyguard unit and expanded into an organization numbering millions, from 1929 to 1945. Himmler controlled Nazi Germany's police and security forces, and was responsible for organizing the systematic **genocide** of Jews, **gypsies**, communists, homosexuals and other condemned groups. Captured by British forces in 1945, he committed suicide by swallowing a cyanide capsule.

Adolf Hitler (1889–1945) was the leader of the German National Socialist (Nazi) Party from 1921 until his death. Within 18 months of his appointment as **Chancellor** of Germany in January 1933, he had destroyed the country's democratic system and established a personal dictatorship with himself as *Führer*, or leader. He restored the German economy and German national pride through **rearmament**, an aggressive determination to retrieve territory lost in World War I, and the **scapegoating** of internal and external enemies. He was primarily responsible for the outbreak of World War II and the subsequent murder of six million Jews in German-occupied Europe. He committed suicide in the *Führerbunker* on 30 April 1945.

Oswald Mosley (1896–1980) served as British Member of Parliament for the Conservative and Labour parties before forming the National Union of Fascists in 1932. This organized several violent rallies in London's East End, but without success. The East Enders rallied to support their Jewish neighbours, and his ideas received little support from the general population. Mosley was imprisoned during World War II.

Benito Mussolini (1883–1945) founded the Italian Fascist Party in 1919 and three years later his threatened March on Rome led to his appointment as Prime Minister. Over the next few years he established a personal dictatorship, with himself cast as *Duce*, or leader. He was at first popular with many Italians, and his army's conquest of Abyssinia in 1935–36 saw this popularity reach its peak. His alliance with Hitler's Germany and Italy's eventual entry into World War II were both deeply unpopular, and his poor military judgement led to a succession of costly defeats. Dismissed and imprisoned by the King of Italy in 1943, he was rescued by German paratroopers and made a **puppet ruler** of a state in northern Italy. In the final weeks of the war he was captured and shot by Italian communist guerrilla fighters.

Glossary

anti-Semitic hostile towards Jews

Austro-Hungarian Empire an empire that covered a large area in Central and Eastern Europe, before 1918

Balilla youth organization for Italian boys in fascist Italy

blue collar worker manual or industrial worker

boycott refusal to have any dealings with a person or organization

cabinet small ruling group

Chancellor in Germany, the prime minister

communism originally an extreme form of socialism, in which property is held communally (in common) rather than by individuals. The term 'communism' became associated with the dictatorial state created in the Soviet Union during the 1920s and 30s.

Communist International an organization formed by the world's communist parties to promote world revolution

concentration camp prison for political prisoners

democracy political system in which governments are regularly elected by the mass of the people

dictatorship government by an individual (called a **dictator**) or a small group that does not allow the mass of the people to have any say in their government

economic sanctions refusal to trade with another nation, either in one particular product or in all products

genocide the deliberate extermination of a people, race or nation

Great Depression period of worldwide economic hardship that lasted throughout most of the 1930s

gypsies a nomadic race of Indian origin. Around 500,000 gypsies were murdered by the Nazis between 1933 and 1945.

ideology a set of ideas on how society should be organized politically and economically

inflation increase in prices or increase in the supply of money (which increases prices)

informer someone who gives information about other people to the authorities

League of Nations international organization founded in 1920 to help settle disputes between nations

left(-wing) in politics, usually associated with policies which place the needs above of the whole community above the short-term wants of the individual

media mass communications like newspapers, radio and TV

nationalism the active promotion of national interest, often at the expense of humanity as a whole

paramilitary semi-official or part-time soldier

parliament a legislative (law-making) assembly which has been at least partly elected

partisans unofficial fighters, against occupying foreign troops

persecute make life difficult for someone

personality cult campaign of exaggerated praise for a person

philosopher thinker about life

plebiscite referendum or direct vote of the whole electorate to a single important political question

propaganda promotion of ideas, often involving a selective version of the truth

puppet ruler ruler who appears to be independent but is actually controlled by the government of another country

racism hatred of other races

reactionary someone who looks to the past for solutions and is resistant to change

rearmament building up supplies of weaponry for armed forces

Reichstag the German parliament

resistance groups groups of unofficial fighters who join together to resist the occupation of their country by another country

revolutionary someone who believes in rapid change rather than gradual progress

Rhineland as laid down in the Treaty of Versailles, a demilitarized zone between the Rhine River and the German border with France, Luxemburg, Belgium and Holland

right(-wing) in politics, usually associated people and policies which favour individual interests over that of the community, freedom over equality, nationalism over internationalism, and traditional values over radical change

SA (Sturmabteilung) stormtroopers: the brown-shirted private army of the National Socialists

scapegoat person or group blamed for other people's shortcomings

socialism a set of political ideas which puts more stress on the needs of the community as a whole and less on the short-term wants or needs of the individual

Spanish Civil War war within Spain (1936–39) between republican government forces (mostly socialists and communists) and rebel forces (mostly conservatives and fascists).

squadristi Italian term for small, organized and unofficial groups of armed men

SS (Schutzstaffel) protection squad: originally Hitler's bodyguard, the black-shirted SS was expanded into a huge organization with both police and military branches led by Heinrich Himmler

Theory of Relativity theory of physics put forward by Albert Einstein in 1905, which enormously advanced human understanding of the way the universe works

totalitarian state a state which demands the obedience of its citizens in all areas of life

trade unions organizations formed to protect and advance the pay and conditions of workers

Treaty of Versailles list of arrangements forced on Germany when it was defeated at the end of World War I

tyranny harsh and undemocratic rule

white collar worker office or professional worker

Index